POCKET ROOM

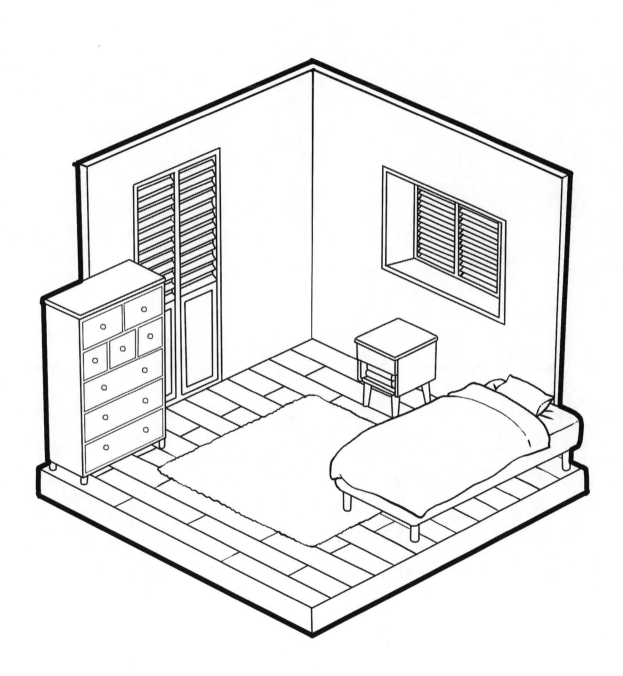

A FEW SINCERE WORDS FOR YOU

We appreciate you picking our coloring book amongst so many others. Your feedback is the highest compliment and source of motivation we could have acquired although we are aware that there are brilliant authors, who have written and released other excellent books.

BEFORE YOU GO

We hope you love our books and would genuinely appreciate it if you could share the sections you colored on social networks with the hashtags: #southernlotus #southernlotuscoloringbook #southernlotuscoloring

In addition, we are eager to read your Amazon reviews. We value all constructive comments, and we'll take them into careful consideration as we work to enhance both our books and our community.

Please feel free to reach out to us if you have any questions.
coloring@southernlotus.com

Visit our social media pages and follow us by using the code below:

This book belongs to:

....

TEST COLOR PAGE

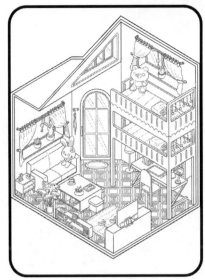

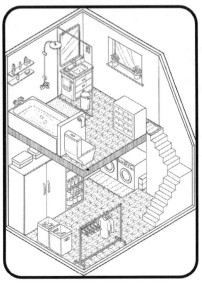

TEST COLOR PAGE

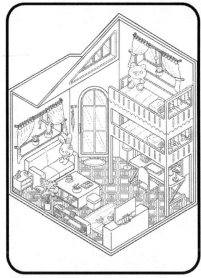

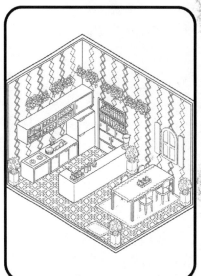

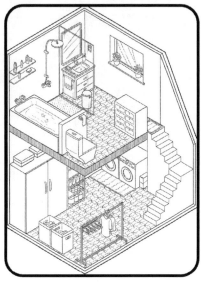

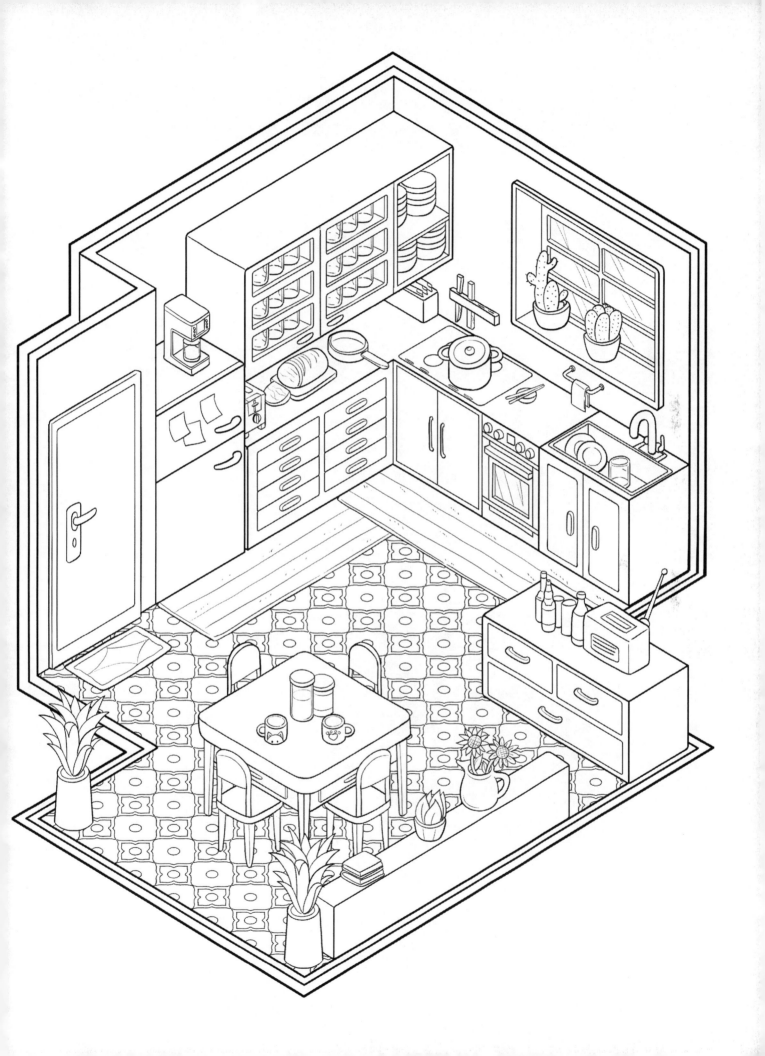

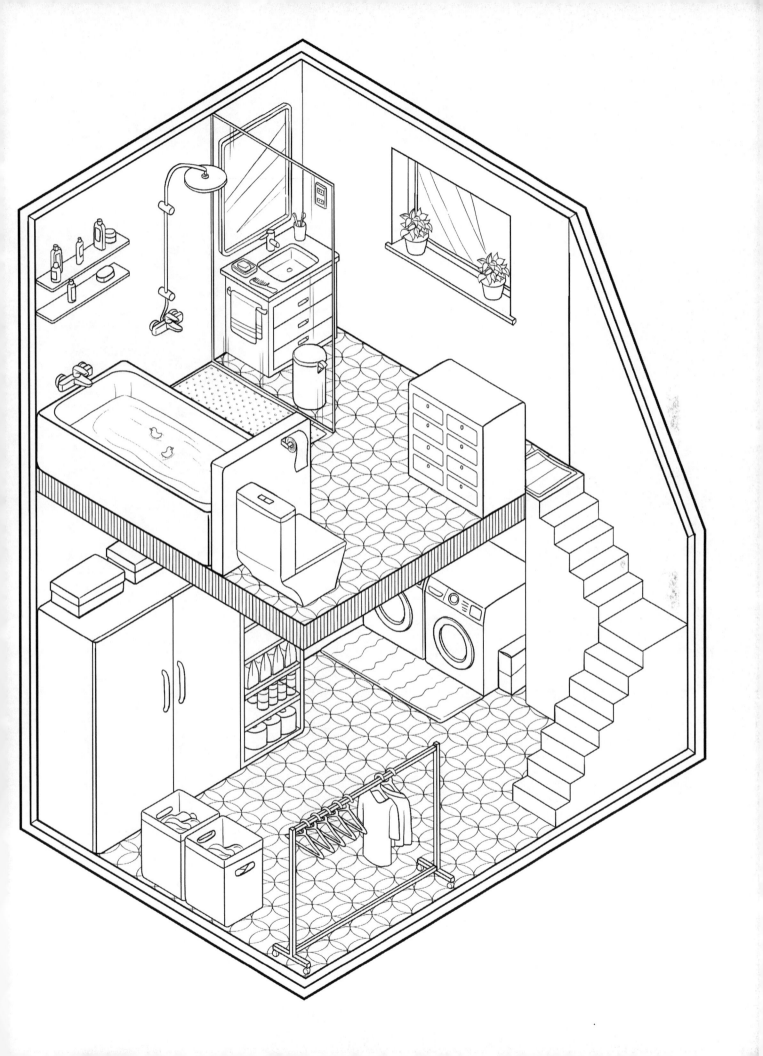

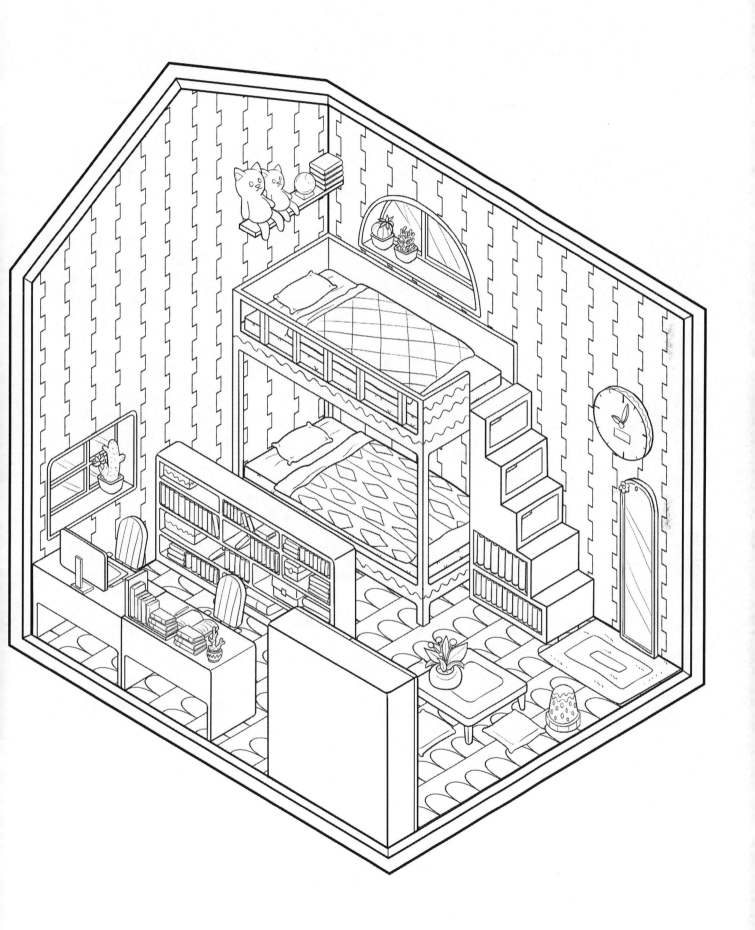

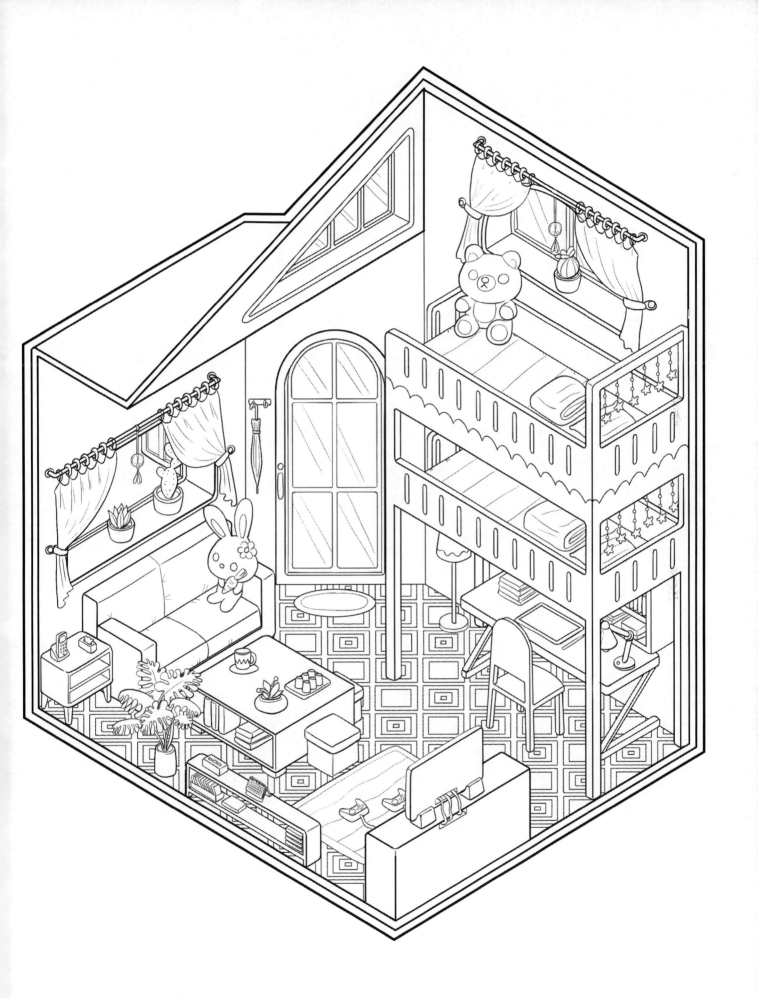

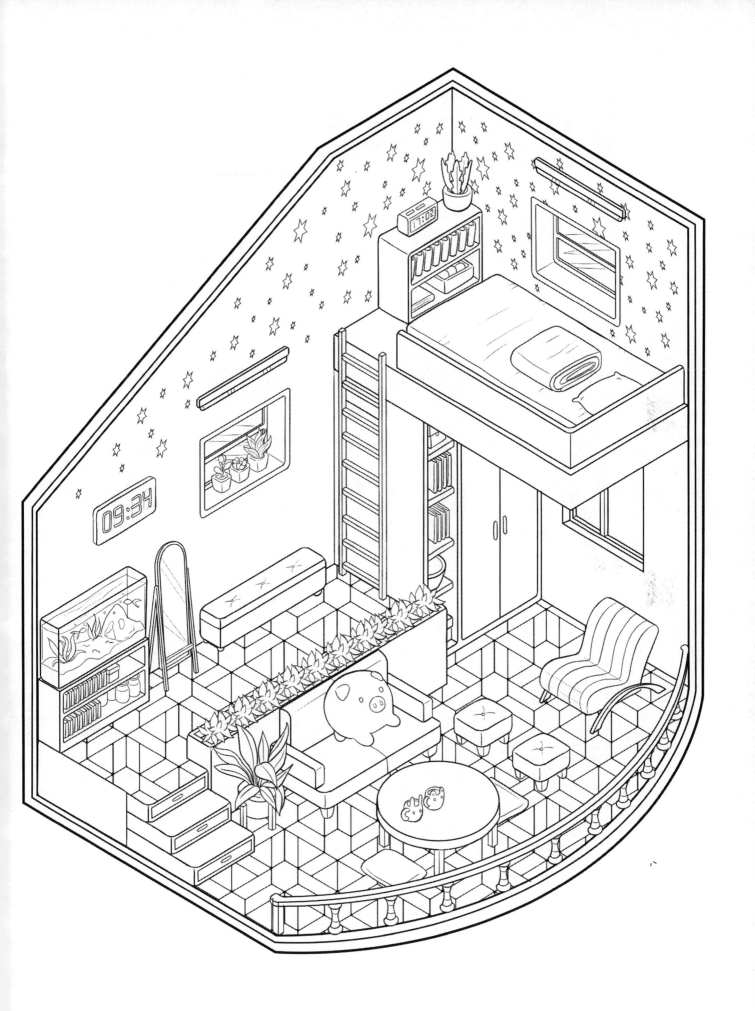

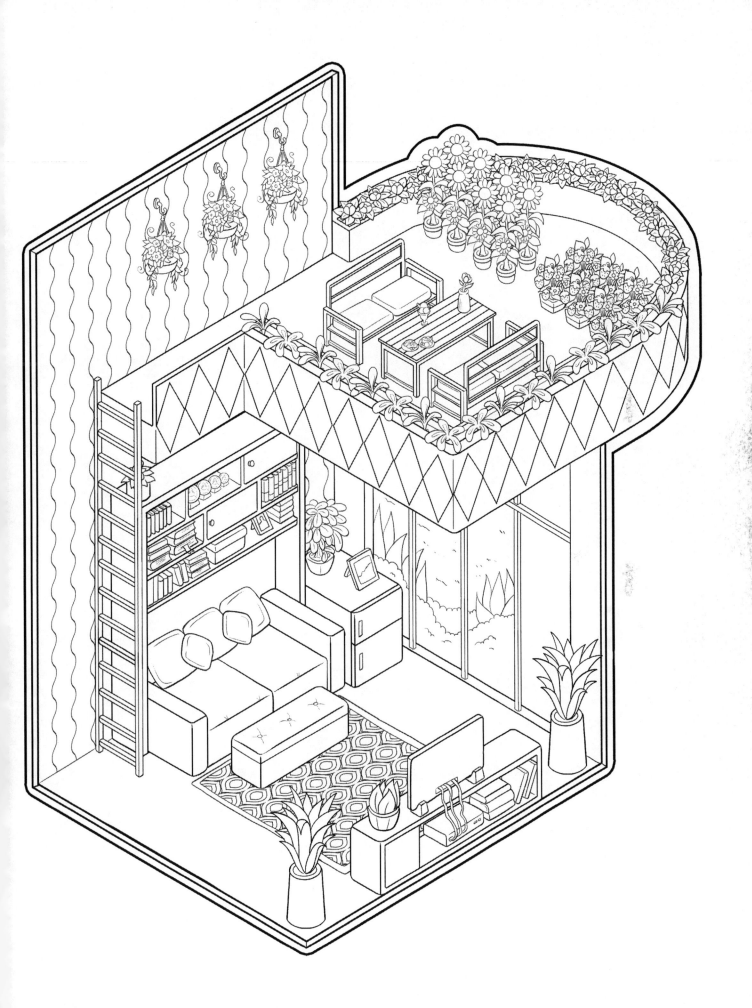

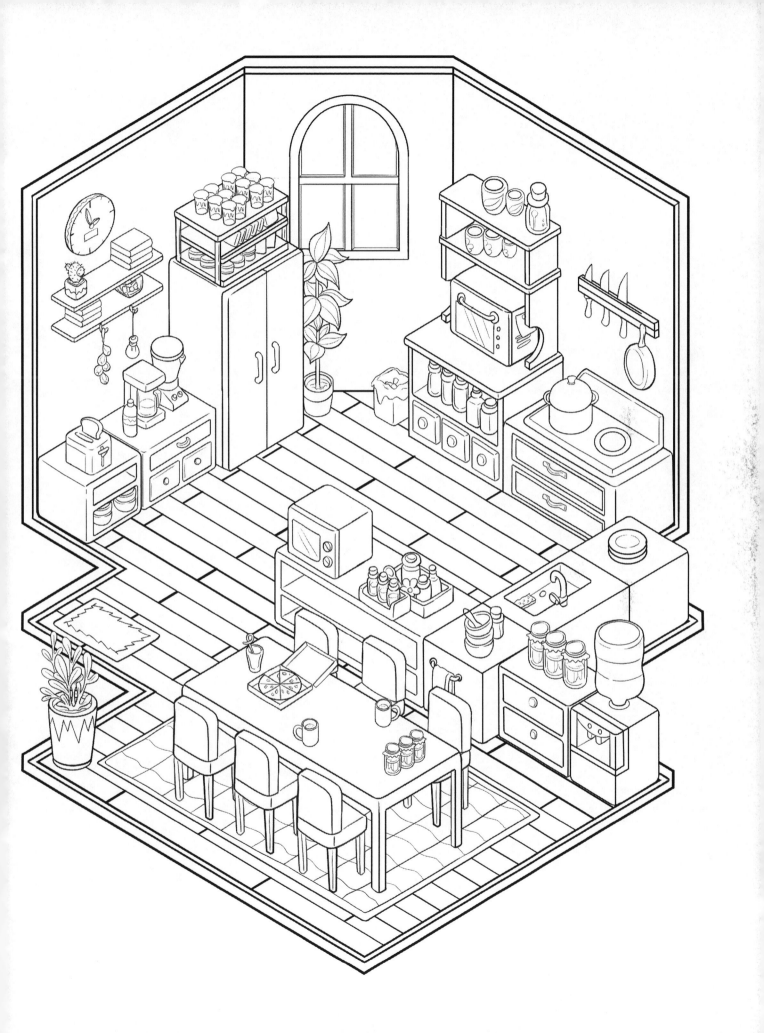

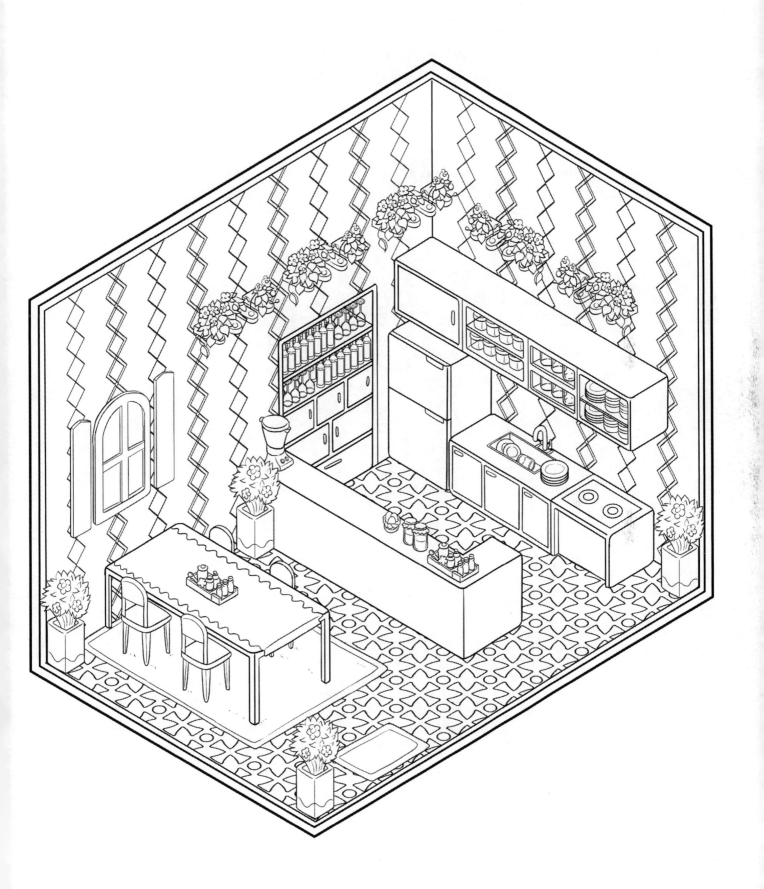

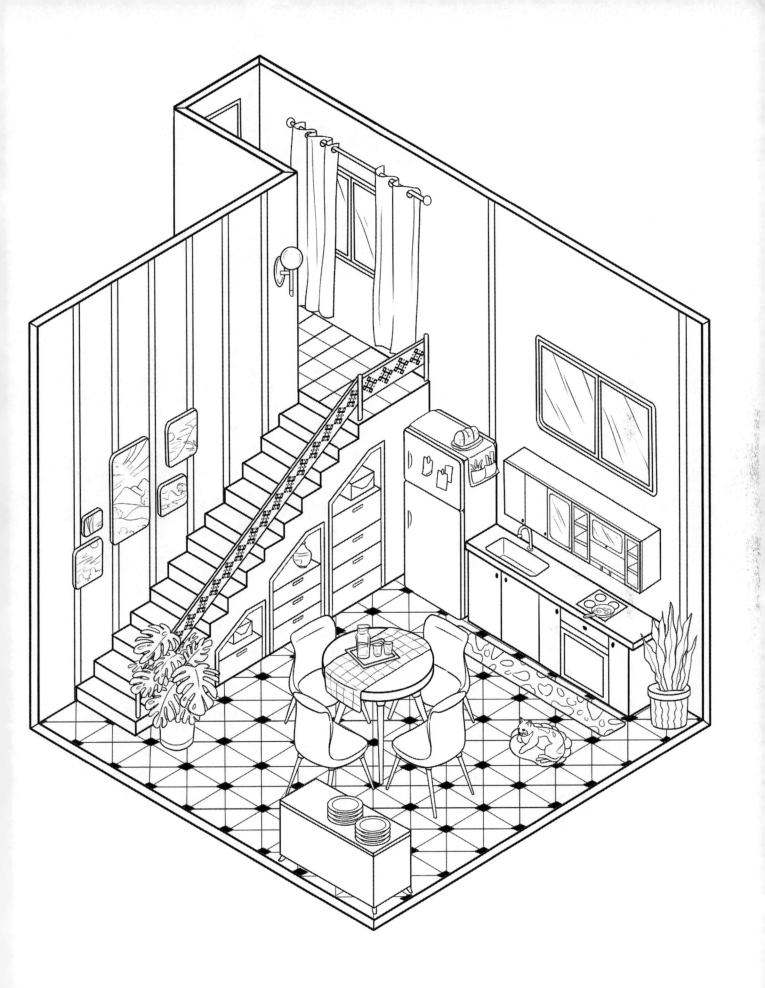

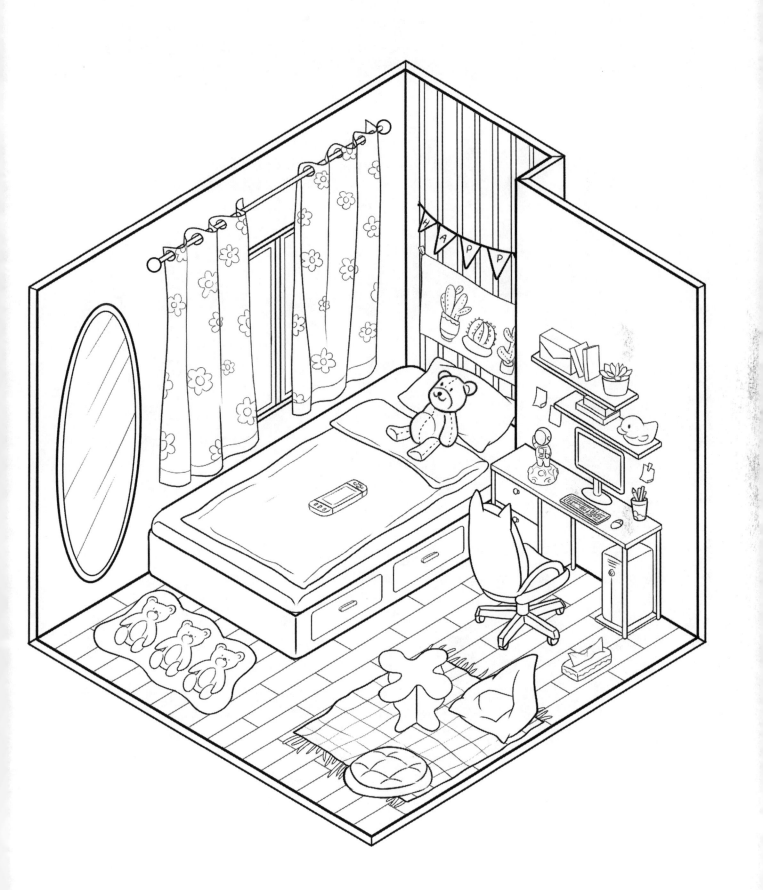

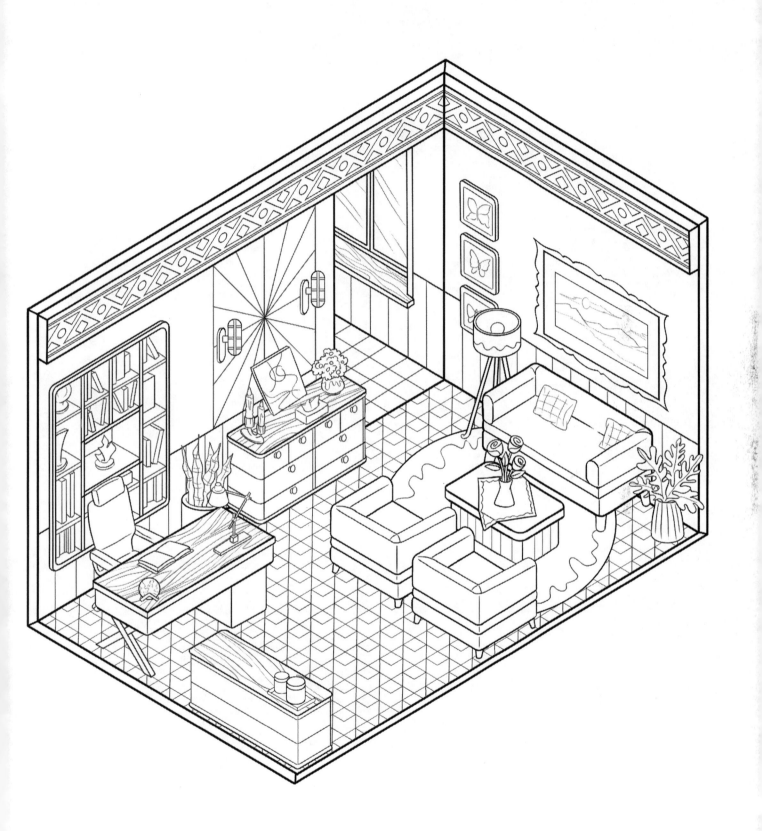

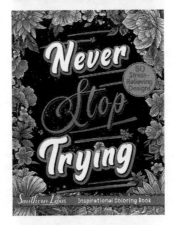

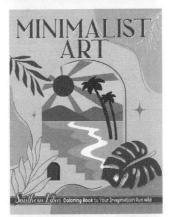

Made in United States
Troutdale, OR
03/15/2024

18500313R00042